CW01653905

Attingham Park
Walled Garden Restoration
A Five Year Diary
2008-2013

Attingham Park
Walled Garden Restoration

A Five Year Diary
2008-2013

First published in 2013 by The Modestine Press

British Library Cataloguing in Publication (CIP) Data.
A catalogue record for this book is available from the British Library.

ISBN 978-1-898720-01-0

Printed by Harlequin Press, Little Horwood
(http://harlequin-press.co.uk)

The Modestine Press
16 Winslow Road
Great Horwood
Milton Keynes MK17 0QN
(http://modestine.co.uk)

Foreword
by Ben Shipston

The restoration of the walled garden at Attingham brings together all that is great about the National Trust: authenticity, the contribution from volunteers, energy and enthusiasm, engagement and passionate commitment – it has been a privilege to be in some small part involved.

Along with stables, pleasure grounds, ice houses, deer parks, water bodies and venerable trees, walled gardens were key components in any 18th Century mansion house. In many ways they are the heartbeat of any working estate, ever changing with the seasons and a hive of activity.

However, it has not always been so at Attingham. When I was fortunate to secure a role with the Trust in 1989, it was with great sadness that I found the walled garden at Attingham was in danger of losing its soul: neglected for many years, in seemingly terminal decline, each passing storm causing the glass houses to slide further into dereliction. Many of its key elements had been lost or were hidden from view and because of the risk, the area was closed off to the public. The main part of the walled garden had been turned over to Christmas tree production and 5,000 trees had been planted. So whilst the skeleton of the garden still survived, the meat had gone and the bones were in danger of crumbling away.

Like the Rediscovered project in the house, the restoration of the walled garden has mirrored the improvements in Attingham's financial fortunes which had been heralded by its huge growth in popularity as a local visitor attraction. The restoration was started first by reversing the years of decline by repairing, reinstating and restoring the buildings, glass houses, paths, dipping ponds and walls. More recently this has been further enhanced and developed thanks to the dedication and sheer hard work of the small team of permanent staff supported by a massive contribution from a loyal band of passionate and skilled volunteers (not forgetting our porcine friends!), and once again the garden is flourishing. The restoration of the walled garden provides a whole new dimension to Attingham and the visitors have shared in the journey through its many stages of restoration. In addition the important link between the garden and the house has been firmly re-established and not only can visitors marvel at the array of fruits and vegetables growing there, but they also have the opportunity to sample them in the tea-room and purchase them to take home.

Who would have imagined when we embarked on this project in the late 1990s that we would have achieved such a wonderful outcome? Certainly the result has far exceeded my expectations and for this I feel all those involved should be justly proud. I hope you take as much pleasure from reading this booklet as I have from watching how the walled garden has risen phoenix-like to take its rightful place once again as one of the key attractions at Attingham.

Ben Shipston
Assistant Director of Operations
National Trust Midland Region

Introduction

Attingham Park's Walled Kitchen Garden was built in the 1780s by Noel Hill, soon to become the first Lord Berwick, of Shrewsbury, Shropshire. Situated on a very slightly sloping south-facing spot around 500 yards from the newly built mansion, its 12 foot high red brick walls surrounded a two acre space of both great beauty and productivity. In its heyday it would have provided the whole household and staff with fruit, vegetables and flowers throughout the year. The latest horticultural technology was deployed to extend the season at both ends, providing the Berwicks with succulent early delicacies from the glass houses and heated walls as well as late ripening autumn fruits in the shade of the north facing wall.

As the Berwicks' fortunes declined the garden adapted to become a market garden supplying local residents, a source of essential foodstuffs during the Second World War "Dig for Victory" campaign, a football field for the adult education college leasing the mansion, and then a Christmas Tree plantation towards the end of the last century. Its glasshouses fell into disrepair, the well and dipping pool were filled with rubble, and the hoggin paths ploughed up. Only the walls remained as a testament to the horticultural excellence that once reigned within (see illustrations, left).

As the 21st Century dawned, it was felt that an attempt should be made to bring the gardens back to life. A request for voluntary help resulted in a very positive response, and Jenny Chandler, Attingham's first "Walled Gardener" was employed to get the ball rolling. She started work on May 19th 2008, the day David Hilditch, local farmer and vintage tractor owner, drove through the double doors at the back of the garden and turned the first soil. From day one she kept up the proud tradition of Head Gardeners through the centuries of keeping a daily log book: noting the weather, tasks carried out and produce harvested. Little did she know that sitting in the mansion archive was the log book of Head Gardener, John Atkinson, begun exactly a century earlier in 1908, and continuing for a full five years. Whilst Jenny moved on to gardens new at the end of her nine-month contract, I arrived in March 2009 to take up the baton. Volunteer numbers increased from twelve to nearly fifty, and the two "seasonal" gardeners, Mary and Deborah, whom I appointed in 2010 are still working hard. Two more part time gardeners are in their second spring in the garden, and we are on to our third annual apprentice from the Women's Farm and Garden Association (a tradition begun by Lady Berwick in 1941 that I was determined to resurrect 70 years on).

The restoration is approaching its fifth birthday so we are reflecting on our progress. With the facsimile of Mr Atknson's log attracting interest from our many visitors it seemed only right to include it in our compilation, contrasting twelve months of his gardening year with our own five year diary. Most days we are a pale reflection of his achievements: he had the advantage of heated greenhouses to produce cucumbers for Christmas and grapes in January. But there was one delicious moment last summer where one of our "Hales Best Jumbo" melons weighed in at 2 1/2 pounds, beating his record by a full 8 ounces.

Selecting the 19th day of each month provides a seasonal snapshot of our horticultural calendar, whilst comparing five years' growth reveals just how far we have come. The log book is quoted verbatim, revealing the highs and lows of any gardener's year. With three quarters of the garden now in full production we have an acre and a half of fruit and vegetables to supply Attingham's restaurants and shop. Three acres of apple orchard can provide a respectable harvest in a good season, producing apples and juice to last us through the year. In 2014 we will be turning the old children's playground back into the "Herbaceous Garden" it once was, providing cut flowers for the mansion, tearoom and shop.

Five acres under full organic production can attract a challenging array of pests which we tackle without Mr Atkinson's chemical armoury; I apologise if the slaughter of said pests seems a recurring theme.

Kate Nicoll
Walled Gardener, May 2013

The Garden in Summer: *May, June and July*

It might seem strange to begin a diary in May, particularly a horticultural diary, when the garden is filling up fast and, all being well, past the danger point of damaging spring frosts. That is when our gardening log begins, however, with Jenny's first day at work, and the all important ploughing of the first quarter. She and the volunteers then had a major catch up task of getting the ploughed earth broken up finely enough to sow the first crops, a job usually done in slow time over the winter months. In subsequent years we have employed pigs rather than ploughs to dig up the next two quarters. In 2010 three Gloucester Old Spots were deployed, working their way around the South East quarter, eating our vegetable trimmings, fertilising the ground and entertaining visitors with their antics. In 2012 we had five Tamworths in the South West quarter, powerful diggers all, but expert escapologists too as Hedley discovered later in the year. May is still early days for harvesting in the kitchen garden: just salads and rhubarb to be picked, although for the first time on May 5th 2012 we had an asparagus crop from the beds planted two years previously. The most productive part of the garden is still the flower borders: the last of the tulips still being cut for the tearoom tables along with the first of the Alliums, Ranunculus and Euphorbias. Crown Imperials back the Bothy Border in the Frame Ground, and the Delphiniums start to fill out the long herbaceous borders through the kitchen garden, hiding the fact that the vegetable beds behind are still relatively sparse.

By June the harvest becomes a lot more varied. The ever popular broad beans are picked by the tray load, kohl rabi, peas, cabbage, beetroot, carrots, and calabrese all get packed into the bicycle trailer and taken down to the shop and tea room. Even the first early potatoes – "Colleen" were ready on June 19th 2011 – along with the first garlic picked while still green and succulent. The bees kept in skeps in the bee house and hives in the orchard are busy pollinating our crops and laying down stores of honey for the winter. They particularly enjoy the crimson clover we grow as a green manure. Technically it should be dug in before flowering but we also enjoy the rich red flowers and always leave at least a strip for the bees. In a good year, Deborah, gardener and bee keeper, extracts the honey to sell at the food fair later in the year. Sweet peas grown along the fence by the old children's playground start to be picked in June, although soon we will have to find a new spot as the area becomes redeveloped as the Herbaceous Garden.

By July the daily sweet pea harvest is no longer a novelty, but has to be done to keep them flowering well. The soft fruit beds also become very productive with red, white and black currants needing to be picked, as well as raspberries and strawberries if we manage to keep the birds and squirrels away. The apricots on the South facing walls begin to ripen, while the peaches and nectarines need thinning and pruning to get the best quality fruit. Weeding becomes a major task, particularly in a wet year. Some days seem to fall into a pattern of harvest all morning and weed all afternoon, with hoeing the preferred method of weed control. The wet weather can lead to a greater risk of potato blight, and although we tend to favour resistant varieties, the few traditional main crops that we grow such as Pink Fir Apple can suffer badly so have to have their foliage removed. Warm days allow us to have our lunch breaks in the orchard, especially good when our volunteer numbers can reach over a dozen, making the Bothy rather crowded.

		£	s	d
1908	To Attingham Hall	£	s	d
May	Brought forward	1	17	5
14	Asparagus^{4} 2 Broccoli^{2} Scotch Kale^{3} Parsley			10
	Lettuce^{1} Mustard & Cress^{1} Radishes^{1} Cucumber^{4}			7
	Onions^{2} Mushrooms^{4} F. Potatoes Strawberries^{9} Rhubarb^{2}		1	8
15	Asparagus^{4} 2 Broccoli^{2} Scotch Kale^{3} Lettuce^{1}			10
	Radishes^{1} Mustard & Cress^{1} Parsley^{1} ½ Cwt Potatoes$^{2/6}$		2	9
	F. Potatoes^{3} Strawberries^{9}		1	
16	2 Asparagus^{8} 1 Dz Broccoli$^{1/-}$ Scotch Kale^{3}		1	11
	Lettuce Mustard & Cress^{1} Parsley^{1} Radishes^{1}			4
	Mushrooms^{6} Carrots^{2} Horseradish^{2} Cucumber^{4}		1	2
	3 Dz Rhubarb^{6} 2 lb F. Potatoes^{6} Strawberries$^{1/-}$		2	
	Nicholls 10 lb Potatoes^{5} Scotch Kale^{2} Rhubarb^{2}			9
18	Scotch Kale^{3} 19th Scotch Kale^{3}			6
20	Scotch Kale^{3} 23rd Broccoli^{4} Lettuce^{1}			8
	Rhubarb^{2} 12 lb Potatoes^{6}			8
27	12 lb Potatoes^{6} 6 Broccoli^{4}			10
29	Asparagus^{3} 2 Broccoli^{2} Lettuce Mustard & Cress			7
	Parsley Mushrooms^{3} F. Potatoes^{3} Strawberries^{6}		1	1
30	2 b. Asparagus^{6} 2 Broccoli^{2} 2 Cabbages^{2}			10
	Lettuce^{1} Mustard & Cress^{1} Mushrooms^{3}			5
	10 lb Potatoes^{5} Frame Potatoes^{2} Strawberries^{9}		1	4
	2 Russell 10 lb Potatoes^{5} Broccoli^{3} Rhubarb^{2}			10
		£ 2	19	0
June 1	1 b. Asparagus^{3} 2 Broccoli^{2} 2 Cabbages^{2}			7
	Frame Potatoes^{2} Strawberries^{6} Flowers^{6}		1	2
3	4 Broccoli^{3} 10 lb Potatoes^{5} Lettuce^{1}			9
	4 Russell 10 lb Potatoes^{5} 4 Broccoli^{3}			8
5	box of Flowers to Hon. Miss Noel-Hill, London		1	
6	2 Cabbages^{2} Lettuce^{2} Cucumber^{3} 10 lb Potatoes^{5}		1	
	Russell 10 lb Potatoes^{5} Cabbage^{2} Lettuce^{1} Cucumber^{3} Rhubarb^{2}		1	2
10	Cabbage^{2} Lettuce^{1} 10 lb Potatoes^{5}			8
	Russell 10 lb Potatoes^{5} Cabbage^{2} Lettuce^{1}			8
	Carried forward		7	8

May 19th 2008 Fine and sunny

Staff: Jenny

Ploughing of first quarter of walled garden @ 9.30am. Several volunteers came along to have a look and also a man from the Shropshire Star. The ploughman was David Hilditch who has a vintage tractor and plough

May 19th 2009 Bright very early, clouding over, showers

Staff: Kate, Jenny; *Volunteers:* Neil, Denise, Diane, John

Slug patrol: collected lots from lettuce in Plot 1, also under pots of squash in greenhouse.

Planted out more "Crystal Lemon" cucumbers and 11 cucumber "Conqueror" in greenhouse. Put up bamboo tripods.

Mad clear up, weed etc in Frame Yard. Finished sweet pea tripods and planting up cutting beds.

Planted last of Cosmos, weeded around trees, hoed paths. Neil made pigeon guards for cauliflowers.

Reorganised Bothy for tea party. Lots of people came including David, the original tractor driver. Liz Roberts made a thank you speech to all the volunteers. I did 2 tours of the garden between showers.

May 19th 2010, Wednesday Humid

Staff: Kate; *Volunteers:* Val, Chris, Peter. Robert

Flowers to tea room: Alliums, Euphorbia and ranunculus.

Val did edges and dug a circle around the Bay tree and put marigolds around. Chris picked flowers for tea room. Robert earthed up all the potatoes and tried to weed kill paths with burner. Chris planted seakale and welsh onions. I watered new peach trees and began fan training with bamboo canes. Peter finished off beehive and made a slab base for it. I seaweed sprayed whole veg garden.

Awful trauma with dog catching 5 chickens in orchard – not killing but wounding! Sam did the deed with one survivor.

May 19th 2011, Thursday Warm and sunny

Staff: Kate and Katherine; *Volunteers:* Wendy, Felicity, Ivor, Ray, Derek, Belinda, Roger, Hannah.

Roger finished shading for bees. Ivor and Ray earthed up potatoes, Katherine sowed three more rows of lettuce in seed bed and planted out another red row in D4. Felicity watered. Belinda weeded alliums and sowed Stoccarde onions. Wendy did all the flowers in the Bothy etc. Weeded roots, thinned carrots, planted more celeriac. Dug out bolted parsley.

Foxtail lilies showing colour, as are apricot and white fox gloves. Iris sibirica splendid,. Blue Delphiniums lovely.

May 19th 2012, Saturday Drizzly and cold most of the day

Fifth anniversary of the starting of the restoration!

Staff: Kate and Deborah; *Volunteers:* Sheila, John, Jean and Heather

10 Bunches Rhubarb to the shop, salads to tea room. China Pink tulips still looking amazing, most others over.

John planted shallot seedlings along edge of A3. Sheila and Heather staked broad beans in C3 and mulched with Composted Green Waste. Deborah planted parsley along edge of herb bed. Kate continued planting annual cut flowers in raised beds and allotment bed (scabious, flax, stocks, zinnias). Sheila planted up veg planter at shop and sowed sunflowers. Jean sowed lots more French Beans in paper pots and potted on aubergines.

May 2008

May 2009

May 2010

May 2011

May 2012

			£	s	d
1908	To Attingham Hall		£	s	d
June	Brought forward	✓		7	8
12	box of Flowers to Hon. Miss Noel-Hill, London			1	
13	Cabbage^{2} Lettuce^{1} Cucumber^{3} 10 lb Potatoes^{5} qt Gooseberries^{4}			1	3
	Russell 10 lb Potatoes^{5} Cabbage^{2} Lettuce^{1} Cucumber^{3} qt Gooseberries^{4}			1	3
17	Cabbage^{2} Lettuce^{1} 10 lb Potatoes^{5}				8
	Russell 10 lb Potatoes^{5} Cabbage^{2} Lettuce^{1}				8
19	box of Flowers to Hon Miss Noel-Hill			1	
20	Cabbage^{2} Lettuce^{1} Cucumber^{3} 10 lb Potatoes^{5} qt Gooseberries^{4}			1	3
	Russell 10 lb Potatoes^{5} Cabbage^{2} Lettuce^{1} Cucumber^{3} Gooseberries^{4}			1	3
24	Cabbage^{2} Lettuce^{1} 10 lb Potatoes^{5}				8
	Russell 10 lb Potatoes^{5} Cabbage^{2} Lettuce^{1}				8
26	box of Flowers to Hon. Miss Noel-Hill			1	
27	1/4 Peas^{3} Cabbage^{2} Lettuce^{1} Cucumber^{3} 10 lb Potatoes^{5}			1	2
	1 qt. Gooseberries^{3}				3
	Russell 10 lb Potatoes^{5} 1/4 Peas^{3} Cabbage^{2}				10
	Lettuce^{1} Cucumber^{3} 1 qt. Gooseberries^{3}				7
		Pd ✓	1	1	2
July 1st	2 Cabbage^{2} Lettuce^{1} 10 lb Potatoes^{5}				8
	2 Russell 10 lb Potatoes^{5} Cabbage^{2} Lettuce^{1}				8
2	6 qts Strawberries			2	
3	Box of Flowers to Hon Miss Noel-Hill			1	
4	1/4 Peas^{3} Cabbage^{2} Lettuce^{1} Cucumber^{3}				9
	6 lb new Potatoes^{6} Rhubarb^{2}				8
	Russell 6 lb Potatoes^{6} 1/4 Peas^{3} Cabbage^{2}				11
	Lettuce^{1} Rhubarb^{2}				3
8	2 Cabbage^{2} Lettuce^{1} 6 lb Potatoes^{6}				9
	Russell 6 lb Potatoes^{6} Cabbage^{2} Lettuce^{1}				9
	4 qts Strawberries			1	4
10	Box of Flowers to Hon. Miss Noel-Hill			1	
11	Cabbage^{2} Lettuce^{1} 1/2 Broad Beans^{4} Cucumber^{3}				10
	6 lb Potatoes^{6} Rhubarb^{2}				8
	Russell 6 lb Potatoes^{6} Cabbage^{2} Lettuce^{1} Cucumber^{3} Rhubarb^{2}			1	2
	Carried forward	✓		13	5

June 19th 2008, Thursday Slight drizzle and very windy

Staff: Jenny; *Volunteers:* Sid

Finished planting Brassicas and netted them all. Also planted more lettuce and spicy mix. Watered beans, potatoes, brassicas and buckwheat.

June 19th 2009, Friday Windy with sunny spells

Staff: Kate

Harvest for shop: Broad beans (5 bags), Mange Tout peas (4 bags), 8 Lettuce, 4 bunches Beetroot.
Harvest for tea room: 25 Lettuce, Sage, Spring Onions, Mange Tout, Parsley and Basil.
Watered tomatoes, pinched out and tied in. Cut back bush tomatoes "Golden Nugget", tasted first one: delicious.

June 19th 2010, Saturday Very pleasant; not too hot

Special event "Food Glorious Food: Lovely Leeks". (Government funded project to encourage sustainable eating: 6 seasonal training days throughout the year ending with the Attingham Feast).
Staff: Deborah, Mary; *Volunteers:* Val, Sheila, Diane, Heather, Neil, Chris and Rob, Wrekin College students
Harvest for shop: Red Russian Kale (5 bunches @ 75p), Lettuce (7 @ 75p), Kohl Rabi (5 @ 75p), Broad Beans (4 bags @ £1), Peas (2 bags @ £1), Sweet peas and, mixed flower bunches (4 bunches @ £2). Harvest for tea room: 8 Lettuce, Strawberries, Spring onions.
Busy setting up for event: several families came in the morning to help plant leeks, fewer for afternoon sessions. Wrekin College came to help weed soft fruit bed, resulting in the loss of a whole currant bush which had to be replanted! Took cuttings from broken branches. Managed some serious weeding elsewhere. Kate also in first thing, finally managed to move the last of the pigs (these had arrived on 15th April to plough up the second quarter of the garden and needed to be moved to the next section – a tricky operation!).

June 19th 2011, Sunday Sunny most of the day

Staff: Kate; *Volunteers:* Sheila, Irene, Martin, Helen, Viv, Ben, Psyche, Connor, David, Julia, Hedley
Harvest for shop: Spring Onions (6 bunches @ 75p), Radish (5 bunches @ 75p), Broad Beans (5 bags @ £1), Peas (8 bags @ £1), Cabbage (6 @ £1) Beetroot (7 bunches @ £1), Carrots (4 bunches @ £1), Potatoes (5 bags "Colleen" @ £1.50), Calabrese (3 heads @ 50p, Garlic (12 heads @ 50p) Raspberries (8 punnets @ £1.50), Sweet peas (2 bunches @ £2).
Harvest for tea room: 1 tray Lettuce, 1 tray mixed leaves and radish.
Still too dry to dig. Tied in sweet peas along espalier railings. Hedley weeded tomato border on South wall, Martin weeded between potatoes, Irene put supports on Chrysanthemums. I started pruning and thinning peaches – lots of fruit very close together.

June 19th 2012, Tuesday Lovely sunny day

Staff: Kate; *Volunteers:* Neil, Ann, Val, Linda, Amanda, Jenny, Sally, Simon, Hannah, Denise
Harvest for shop: Broad Beans (14 bags @ £1), Lettuce (6 @ £1), Spinach (5 bags @ 75p, Strawberries (6 punnets @ £1), Nigella and Euphorbia (10 bunches @ £2)
Harvest for tea room: 2 trays Lettuce, 1 tray mixed leaves.
Neil tied in rest of wall tomatoes and watered all greenhouses and pots. Thorough weed in D3. Val finished weeding spinach under bean arch. Denise weeded bindweed out of new asparagus bed. Sally weeded allium bed and thinned young onions. Amanda removed bolted lettuce from A2 and fed to the pigs. Planted out new lettuce with Jenny. Ann edged grass paths all day, helped by Linda. Simon harvested then finished putting canes in Melon House to support melons and cucumbers, also planted statice in raised beds. I planted annuals in Bothy bed and weeded. Sally and Amanda pulled all spent tulip heads out of allotment cutting bed.

June 2008

June 2009

June 2010

June 2011

June 2012

A

		£	s	d
1908	To Attingham Hall	£	s	d
July	Brought forward		13	5
15	1/4 Peas ^{3} Cabbage ^{2} Lettuce ^{1} 6 # Potatoes ^{6}		1	
	Russell 6 # Potatoes ^{6} Cabbage ^{2} Lettuce ^{1}			9
18	1 Cabbage ^{2} Lettuce ^{1} 6 # Potatoes ^{6}			9
	1 Cucumber ^{3}, 1 qt Blk Currants ^{3}			6
	Russell 6 # Potatoes ^{6} Cabbage ^{2} Lettuce ^{1}			9
	Cucumber ^{3} 1 qt Blk Currants ^{3}			6
21	4 qt Blk. Currants 1/-		1	0
22	Cabbage ^{2} Lettuce ^{1} 6 # Potatoes ^{5} Onions ^{2} Herbs ^{1}			11
	Russell 6 # Potatoes ^{5} Cabbage ^{2} Lettuce ^{1}			8
24	Box of Flowers to Hon Miss Noel-Hill		1	
25	1/4 Peas ^{3} Lettuce ^{1} Cucumber ^{3} 6 # Potatoes ^{5}		1	
	Raspberries & Currants ^{5}			5
	Russell 6 # Potatoes ^{5} 1/4 Peas ^{3} Lettuce ^{1} Rasp. & Currants ^{5}		1	2
27	5 qt Raspberries 1/- 3 qts Red Currants 9		1	9
29	1/2 Broad Beans ^{4} Lettuce ^{1} 6 # Potatoes ^{5}			10
	Russell 6 # Potatoes ^{5} 1/2 B Beans ^{4} Lettuce ^{1}			10
31	Box of Flowers to Hon Miss Noel-Hill		1	
		1	8	3
August 1st	1/4 Peas ^{3} Lettuce ^{1} 7 # Potatoes ^{6} 1 Cucumber ^{3} 1 qt Red Currants ^{2}		1	3
	– Russell 7 # Potatoes ^{6} 1/4 Peas ^{3} Lettuce ^{1} Cucumber ^{3} 1 qt Red Currants ^{2}		1	3
5	1/4 Peas ^{3} Lettuce ^{1} 6 # Potatoes ^{5}			9
	– Russell 6 # Potatoes ^{5} Lettuce ^{1} Cabbage ^{2}			8
7	– Box of Flowers to Hon Miss Noel-Hill		1	
8	– 1/4 Peas ^{3} Lettuce ^{1} Cucumber ^{3} 6 # Potatoes ^{5} 1 qt Plums ^{3}		1	3
	Russell 6 # Potatoes ^{5} Lettuce ^{1} Cucumber ^{3} 1/4 Peas ^{3} 1 qt Plums ^{3}		1	3
12	1 Vegetable Marrow ^{3} Lettuce ^{1} 7 # Potatoes ^{5}			9
	– Russell 7 # Potatoes ^{5} Lettuce ^{1} 1 Vegetable Marrow ^{3}			9
14	– Box of Flowers to Hon Miss Noel-Hill		1	
15	1/4 R. Beans ^{2} Lettuce ^{1} Cucumber ^{3} Onions ^{2} Herbs ^{2}			10
	10 # Potatoes ^{6} 1/4 Apples ^{2}			8
	– Russell 7 # Potatoes ^{4} 1/4 R. Beans ^{2} Lettuce ^{1} Cucumber ^{3} 1/4 Apples ^{2}		1	
	Carried forward		12	5

July 19th 2008, Saturday

Staff: Jenny

Planted out last egg plants in free standing green house. Tidied tomatoes, took out laterals, tied in and watered.

July 19th 2009, Sunday Overcast with some heavy showers

Staff: Jenny

Harvest for shop: Chard (3 bunches @ 75p), Kale (4 bunches @ 75p) Rhubarb (4 bunches @ £1) Parsley (3 bunches @ 50p) Sorrel (3 bunches @ 50p).

Harvest for tea room: Spring onions (large bunch)

Finished wildlife hotel, attached tiles to the side, dug into ground and grouted with silicone. Planted gourds and beans. Sowed carrots, radish, swede, rainbow chard, lettuce, spring onions and borecole. Surprising number of visitors about in the afternoon.

July 19th 2010, Monday

Staff: Deborah

Harvest for tea room: 9 Lettuce (mixed red and green), New potatoes (2.5kg), ½ tray Basil, ½ tray raspberries, 1 large bunch Beetroot, small bunch Rocket.

Watered greenhouses, fed animals and general catch up after a week's holiday. Paperwork and email in the office. Some visitors – all very complimentary.

July 19th 2011, Tuesday

Staff: Kate and Deborah; *Volunteers:* Neil, Hannah, Ann, Amanda, Sally, Val

Harvest for shop: Beetroot (10 bunches @ £1), Baby Carrots (6 bunches @ 75p) Anya Potatoes (4 1kg bags @ £1.50), Florence Fennel (5 bulbs @ £1), Globe Artichokes (5 @ 50p), Marrow (1 @ £1), "Alderman" Peas (9 bags @ £1), Calabrese (9 bags @ £1), Spring Onions (5 bunches @ 75p), Plums (3 punnets @ £2).

Harvest for tea room: 1 tray Lettuce, 1 bunch Spring Onions.

Neil weeded wall borders to remove bindweed. Amanda and Sally removed bolted lettuce in D4 and sowed Hungarian Rye. Val weeded circular flower borders. Ann weeded onions. Hannah tidied up after Kohl Rabi and planted a row of White Broccoli. I weeded Pear Borders. Sally thinned carrots and covered with Enviromesh against carrot root fly.

July 19th 2012, Thursday Dry with a slight shower midday

Staff: Kate, Mary, Gaye (WFGA apprentice); *Volunteers:* Chris, Tony, Ivor, Ray, John, Roger, Felicity, Val

Harvest for shop: Lettuce (6 @ £1), Beetroot (6 bags @ £1), Carrots (6 bunches @ £1) Baby Parsnips (4 bags @ £1), Tomatoes and Basil (3 bags @ £1.50), Cucumbers (4 @ £1), Crystal Lemon Cucumbers (5 @ 50p), Anya Potatoes (5 bags @ £1.50)

Harvest for tea room: 1 tray Lettuce, 1 tray Mixed Leaves, 6 punnets Raspberries, 1kg Dessert Gooseberries, 1 tray Courgettes, ½ tray Cherry Tomatoes, 1 tray Broad Beans.

Big harvest of soft fruit in B4, then Gaye weeded. Ivor lifted autumn sown onions in B4 (Cippola – none firm enough to store, quite a lot of rot). Roger mowed paths and labyrinth and put up photos in Bothy. Ray dug Charlotte potatoes and cleared foliage off more (blight now spreading). Tony forked over A1 ready for green manure sowing. I planted chicory in D1 and weeded bolted lettuce for pigs. Mary tidied tomatoes indoor and out.

Lunch party for Gaye's last day. Lovely Walled Garden cake made by Margaret, plus assorted savouries. Gave her a veg box, plus a bunch of flowers with 48 different varieties of flowers! She gave us a lovely boot scraper for outside the Bothy door.

July 2008

July 2009

July 2010

July 2011

July 2012

The Garden in Autumn:
August, September and October

Although August is not usually regarded as autumnal it marks the turning point when the kitchen garden begins to empty out as the harvest continues and it is too late to plant anything out apart from salads. The annual cut flowers are still providing plenty of colour, particularly the tender annuals such as Tithonia or Mexican Sunflowers. The herbaceous borders begin to quieten down as the first flush goes over and they get trimmed back in the hope of a second flowering. That is when the iron railings are revealed again, with their planting of espaliered pear trees trained horizontally against the bars. We started installing the railings in 2010 after finding photographs in the mansion archive of a similar arrangement in the 1930s. They both provide a structure on which to train the pears, and give the garden the extra dimension of height, particularly important in the winter when the empty garden can begin to resemble a ploughed field. The walls too are an essential area for training fruit, indeed that was one of their main functions. Each aspect favours a particular type of fan trained tree. Morello cherries grow well on the North facing wall, whilst sweet cherries require the warmth of facing West. Peaches, apricots and nectarines ripen best on the South facing wall, while plums, gages and damsons do well facing East. It has taken us five years to get all 50 trees back on to the wall and it will take a further decade for them to clothe the walls fully.

During the summer holidays the gardens are often visited by children who love to get involved in a practical task. Watering is especially popular, with our Victorian water cart used for dipping child sized watering cans which are then taken off around the garden. The glass houses need daily watering as they fill up with tender crops such as peppers, tomatoes, aubergines and melons. Outside we start lifting the onion crop to dry off before storing for winter. The sweet corn starts to ripen and we try to pick the globe artichokes before they open to reveal themselves as the overgrown thistles they really are. By September the piglets that arrived as weaners back in April are fully grown, feasting on the windfall apples as well as any vegetables that are past their prime. As they grow they become increasingly less biddable, and moving them from one section to another becomes more of a performance. The electric fence is all-important to fend them off digging up the grass paths between the beds. When the battery died overnight we all discovered the next morning just how determined they were to plough up pastures new. Luckily Home Farm's long horn cattle have only managed to break in through the double doors a few times since the restoration began. However, as we fill up more and more with tasty vegetable crops the prospect gets increasingly enticing for them and worrying for us.

By October most of the 37 varieties of apples in the orchard have ripened and are ready to be picked. We store all those that appear to be perfect on wooden racks in the apple store. In theory these should keep in good condition right through to the following spring. In practice, however, an old orchard run on organic principles produces plenty of slightly imperfect fruit that are ideal to turn into apple juice. We do this using our apple press made of oak. If we make more than can be consumed on the day by visitors to our popular Harvest Fair, we preserve it either by freezing or pasteurising it. This can then be turned into delicious mulled apple juice for our winter events such as the Frost Fair or Candlelit snowdrop evenings. Other fruits are also ready this month: the "Shropshire Prune" or damson sells well in the shop, pears are turned into pear tarts by the tea room, whilst the Medlar needs another month to ripen before being turned into jams and jellies.

1908	To Attingham Hall	£	s	d
August	Brought forward		12	5
18	1/4 Peas 3 1/4 R. Beans 2 Lettuce 1 Parsley 1 2 lb Tomatoes 8		1	3
	1¼ lb Grapes 1/3 Plums 2 Apples 2 Flowers 6 Cucumbers 3		2	4
	3 Doz Apricots 3/-		3	
19	1/2 Peck French Beans 4 2 Cauliflowers 2 Lettuce 1 10 lb Potatoes 6		1	1
	6 Peaches 1/6 Plums 3 1 lb Grapes 1/-		2	9
	- Russell 1/4 Peas 3 Lettuce 1 7 lb Potatoes 4			8
20	6 Peaches 1/3 1¼ lb Grapes 1/3 Flowers 3		2	9
22	1/4 R. Beans 2 Lettuce 1 Cucumbers 1 10 lb Potatoes 6 1 qt Plums 3		1	3
	- Russell 1/4 R. Beans 2 Lettuce 1 Cucumbers 3 10 lb Potatoes 6 1 qt Plums		1	3
26	10 lb Potatoes 5 Lettuce 1 1 Vegetable Marrow 3			9
	- Russell 10 lb Potatoes 5 Lettuce 1 1 Vegetable Marrow 3			9
29	1/4 Peas 3 Lettuce 1 Cucumbers 3 10 lb Potatoes 5 1 qt Plums 3		1	3
	Russell 10 lb Potatoes 5 1/4 Peas 3 Lettuce 1 Cucumbers 3 1 qt Plums 3		1	3
31	12 qts Plums		3	
		£ 1	15	9
September	1/2 Peck Broad Beans 3 2 Cauliflowers 2			5
2	Lettuce 1 10 lb Potatoes 5			6
	2 Russell 10 lb Potatoes 5 2 Cauliflowers 2 Lettuce 1			8
	1/2 B. Beans 3 4 qts Plums 6			9
5	1/4 R. Beans 2 Lettuce 1 Cucumbers 3			6
	10 lb Potatoes 5 1 qt Plums 2			7
	- Russell 10 lb Potatoes 5 1/4 R. Beans 2 Lettuce 1			8
	Cucumbers 3 1 qt Plums 2			5
7	1/4 Peas 3 1/4 R. Beans 2 Lettuce 1 Parsley 1			7
	2 lb Tomatoes 6 1 lb Grapes 1/4 1 Melon 6		2	4
	6 Peaches 1/- Radishes 1 Flowers 6		1	7
8	Cabbage 2 Plums 2 Apples 2 2½ lb Grapes 3/-		3	6
9	1/4 R. Beans 2 2 Cauliflowers 2 Mushrooms 2			6
	6 Peaches 1/- Grapes 1/-		2	
	- Russell 10 lb Potatoes 5 Cabbage 2 Lettuce 1			8
10	1 lb 10 oz Grapes 2/5 Box of Flowers 1/-		3	5
	Carried forward	£	19	1

August 18th 2008, Monday Overcast and humid with occasional drizzle

(August 19th Mule driving Course)

Staff: Jenny

Harvest for shop: Beetroot, Courgettes, Chard, Kale, Radish, Dahlias.

Harvest for tea room: 1 tray Lettuce, 1 tray Herbs (Basil, Parsley, Sage, Thyme, Oregano), Tomatoes, French Beans and Radish.

Pulled out almost all tomatoes to burn because of blight. Saved green fruit for tea room to make chutney. Picked caterpillars off brassicas and put onto bird feeders. Fed plants in greenhouse with comfrey tea.

August 19th 2009, Tuesday

Staff: Kate; *Volunteers:* Val, John.

Harvest for shop: Broad Beans (18 bags @ £1), Arran Victory Potatoes (3 bags @ £1), Tomatoes 8 bags @ £1), Runner Beans (10 bags @ £1), Borlotti Beans (2 bags @ £1), Blue Coco French Beans (3 bags @ £1), Dwarf French Beans (2 bags @ £1).

Harvest for tea room: 1 tray mixed Lettuce, ½ Courgettes, ½ tray rocket and red mustard, bunch of chives.

Cut back last of Broad Beans (Express) and picked 9kg to sell. Cleared section and forked over. John dug half a row of Arran Victory potatoes. Val edged grass path.

August 19th 2010, Thursday

Staff: Kate, Mary, Deborah, Katherine; *Volunteers:* Roger, Ann, Ivor, Derek, Andrea, Julia, David, Alex, Ray

Harvest for shop: Chard (6 bunches @ 75p), Runner beans (3 bundles @ £1), Purple Runner Beans (13 bundles @ £1), Beetroot (3 bunches @ £1), Kohl Rabi (4 @ 50p) Crystal Lemon Cucumber (3 @ 75p, Cucumbers (4 @ £1), Climbing French Beans (4 bags @ £1), mixed flowers (4 Bunches @ £2).

Harvest for tea room: 1 tray Courgettes, 1 tray mixed lettuce, 1 tray rocket and red mustard, bunch of chives.

Derek and Ray dug new curved flower border in the pig quarter. Ann and Ivor weeded path edges. Andrea potted up iris bulbs. Roger continued labelling apple trees with engraved aluminium labels.

August 19th 2011, Friday Sunny and still dry, lots of visitors

Staff: Mary

Harvest for shop: Runner beans (9 bundles @ £1), Beetroot (2 bunches @ 75p), Cucumbers (6 @ 50p, Victoria plums (8 punnets @ £2), Peaches (3 punnets @ £2), Nectarines (2 punnets @ £2), Lettuce (2 @ 75p), Blue Coco Beans (6 bags @ £1), Amorosa and Setanta Potatoes (7 bags @ £1.50).

Harvest for tea room: ½ tray Chard, 1 tray mixed lettuce, radish and raspberries.

Harvesting most of the day, including a display for Victorian Kitchen in the mansion. Glass house work: removing melon and cucumber leaves showing signs of red spider mite.

August 19th 2012, Sunday Sunny morning and afternoon, rain at midday

Staff: Kate; *Volunteers:* Hedley, Sheila, Helen, John

Harvest for shop: Runner beans (20 bags @ £1), French Beans (14 bags @ £1), Beetroot (12 bags @ £1), Courgettes (9 @ 50p), Marrow (1 @ £1), Crystal Lemon Cucumbers (6 @ 50p)

Harvest for tea room: 1 tray mixed lettuce.

Drama with pigs escaping due to flat battery. Poor Hedley had to try to fend them off digging up the grass paths until new battery was ready. Sheila, Helen and John weeded C3 and B3 – looks great. I continued cutting back and weeding in Pear borders. Picked a 2½lb melon – beating Mr Atkinson in the old log book.

August 2008

August 2009

August 2010

August 2011

August 2012

		£	s	d
1908	To Attingham Hall	£	s	d
September	Brought forward		19	1
12	1/4 R. Beans 2 2 Cauliflowers 2 Lettuce 1 Cucumbers 3			8
	10 lb Potatoes 5 1 qt Plums 2			7
	- Russell 10 lb Potatoes 5 2 Cauliflowers 2 Lettuce 1			8
	Cucumbers 3 1 qt Plums 2			5
15	1/4 Peas 3 2 Cauliflowers 2 1 Cabbage 2 Lettuce 1			8
	Onions 2 Herbs 2 Mustard & Cress 1 6 Peaches 1/-		1	5
	6 Pears 2 3/4 lb Grapes 1/- 1 Melon 6		1	8
16	1/4 Peas 3 1/4 R. Beans 2 2 Cauliflowers 2 Cabbage 2			9
	Lettuce 1 Mustard & Cress 1 10 lb Potatoes 5 2 lb Tomatoes 6		1	1
	6 Nectarines 6 6 Apples 2 3/4 lb Grapes 1/-		1	8
	- Russell 10 lb Potatoes 5 Cabbage 2 Lettuce 1			8
18	1/2 Cwt Potatoes 1/6 1 Peck Apples 10		2	4
19	1/2 Peas 3 1/4 R Beans 2 2 Cauliflowers 2 Cabbage 2			9
	Lettuce 1 Parsley 1 Mustard & Cress 1 Cucumbers 3			6
	2 lb Tomatoes 6 4 qt Damsons 8		1	2
	6 Peaches 1/- 6 Pears 3 1 Melon 6 3/4 lb Grapes 1/- Flowers 6		3	3
	- Russell 10 lb Potatoes 5 Cabbage 2 Lettuce 1			8
	Cucumbers 3 1 qt Damsons 2			5
	Fruit Flowers & Vegetables to Atcham Church		2	6
21	1/4 Peas 3 2 Cauliflowers 2 Lettuce 1 Mustard & Cress 1			7
	Radishes 1 1 Peck R. Beans 6 6 Nectarines 6		1	1
	Apples 2 3/4 lb Grapes 1/-		1	2
22	1/4 R. Beans 2 6 Beetroots 6 6 Peaches Plums 2 Grapes 1/-		1	10
23	1/4 Peas 3 2 lb Tomatoes 6 Lettuce Mustard & Cress Flowers 6		1	5
	Russell 10 lb Potatoes 5 Cabbage 2			7
	Lettuce 1 4 qt Damsons 8			9
24	1/4 Peas 3 2 Cauliflowers Radishes 1 Lettuce 1			7
	Parsley 1 Cabbage 2 6 Figs 6 6 Pears 4 1 lb Grapes 1/4		2	5
25	1/4 Peas 3 1/4 R. Beans 2 2 Vegetable Marrows 4			9
	Cucumbers 2 Lettuce 1 Parsley 1 2 lb Tomatoes 6			11
	6 Nectarines 6 1 lb Grapes 1/4 1 Melon 6 6 Figs 6 1/2 Cwt Potatoes 1/6		4	4
	Carried forward	£ 2	17	4

September 20th 2008, Saturday Chilly start, very heavy dew, only 9 degrees, then sun came out, beautiful warm day

Volunteers: Sheila
Harvest for shop: Runner Beans, French Beans, Beetroot, Chard.
Harvest for tea room: 1 tray mixed Lettuce, Salad Leaves and Radish.
Watered greenhouse. Weeding and caterpillar squashing. Some whitefly on aubergines. Plenty of visitors in the garden, glad to see it being used again.

September 19th 2009 Saturday Chilly start then warm and sunny

Volunteers: Sheila, Mary
Harvest for food fair: Damsons, Leeks, Runner beans, Courgettes, Garlic, Shallots, Pumpkins, Flowers

September 19th 2010 Sunday Wet start, dry later, many visitors

Staff: Mary; *Volunteers:* Hedley
Harvest for shop: Runner beans (9 bunches @ £1), Purple French Beans (6 bags @ 75p), Borlotti Beans (2 bags @ £1), Tuscan Kale (3 bunches @ 75p), Chard (5 bunches @ 75p), Sweet peas (6 bunches @ £2), Mixed flowers (2 bunches @ £2)
Six eggs
Harvest for tea room: 1 tray mixed lettuce.
Hedley collected windfall apples, watered greenhouses, lit a fire and did a grand job of tidying up the potato bed after yesterday's activity (Food Glorious Food harvesting day for visitors). Put the potatoes (Valor and Sarpo Mira) in the vinery to dry off before storing.

September 19th 2011 , Monday Cloudy and cool; very quiet

Staff: Kate, Deborah
Harvest for tea room: 1 tray Basil
Watered beans, roots and box cuttings as still very dry. Sorted out plants on Standing out area. Statice in bud again after being cut back. Caught up with office work.

September 19th 2012, Wednesday Some sun, some cloud, warm

Staff: Belinda, Jenny (WFGA apprentice); *Volunteers:* Jenny, Marion, Peter, Rosemarie, Chris, Rob, Kathleen and Sylvia.
Harvest for shop: Courgettes (6 @ 50p), Dwarf French Beans (2 bags @ £1), Climbing French Beans 6 bags @ £1), Leeks (13 @ 50p), Custard Marrows (5 @ 75p), Runner Beans (7 bags @ £1), Sweet corn (12 @ £1), Damsons (14 bags @ £1).
Harvest for tea room: 1 tray Leeks, 3 punnets Raspberries, 3 punnets Blackberries, 1 tray Tomatoes, 1 tray windfall Cooking Apples.
Marion harvested Damsons, dug over Allium bed, fed pigs with veg scraps. Peter mowed back borders and weeded. Rob weeded and helped Chris cut down fennel in herb bed. Kathleen harvested and changed flowers in Bothy. Sylvia harvested soft fruit, dead headed etc. Jenny harvested and sowed grazing rye as green manure in A2.
Belinda prepared B1 for spring cabbage planting, damped down greenhouses, cut flowers for house and tea room.

September 2008

September 2009

September 2010

September 2012

September 2011

1908	To Attingham Hall	£	s	d
October	Brought forward	3	2	7
17	1/4 Peas[3] 2 Cauliflower[2] Lettuce[1] Cucumber[3]			9
	1/2 Peck Apples[4] 1/4 Apples[2]			6
	– Russell 10 lb Potatoes[5] Cabbage[2] Lettuce[1] Cucumber[3]			10
20	1/2 Peck Apples[4]			4
21	3 small Savoys[2] Lettuce[1]			3
	to Russell 10 lb Potatoes[5] Savoys[2] Lettuce[1]			8
23	Box of Flowers to Hon. Miss Noel-Hill			6
24	1/4 Peas[3] 1 Vegetable Marrow[2] Lettuce[1] 1/4 Apples[2]			8
	1/2 Cwt Potatoes[1/6] Cucumber[3]		1	9
	– Russell 10 lb Potatoes[5] Cabbage[2] Lettuce[1]			8
	Cucumber[3] 1/4 Apples[2]			5
28	2 Savoys[2] Lettuce[1]			3
	Russell 10 lb Potatoes[5] Savoys[2] Lettuce[1]			8
30	Box of Flowers to Hon Miss Noel-Hill			8
31	2 Cauliflower[2] Cabbage[1] Lettuce[1] Cucumber[2] 1/4 Apples[2]			8
	– Russell 10 lb Potatoes[5] Cabbage[3] Lettuce[1] Cucumber[2] 1/4 Apples[2]		1	1
	£	3	13	3

October 19th 2008, Sunday
No staff, no volunteers.

October 19th 2009, Monday Sunny and mild
Staff: Kate
Harvest for shop: Curly Kale (4 bunches @ 50p), Parsley (4 bunches @ 50p), Swiss Chard (4 bunches @ 50p), Runner Beans (3 Bunches @ 50p), Courgettes (4 @ 50p), Peppers (4 bags @ 50p), Butternut Squash (3 @ £1).
Harvest for tea room: 1 tray Tomatoes and Basil, 8 Conference Pears, 1 string Garlic.
Did harvest: last of Runner Beans and Courgettes, I think. Collected barrowload of wood ash from riverside. Fed strawberry patch with Fish, Blood and Bone, top dressed with wood ash. Mulched whole bed with Composted Green Waste (from Telford and Wrekin Council), as going to be wet and windy tomorrow. Filled gaps in wild strawberries with last of our plants grown from seed. Willow (my Labrador) caught a grey squirrel in the Orchard!

October 19th 2010, Tuesday Bright morning, very heavy showers in the afternoon
Staff: Mary,; *Volunteers:* Neil, Val, Denise, Dave, 3 Work Experience Students (Freda, Will and Elaine).
Harvest for shop: Celeriac (6 @ £1), Curly Kale (3 bunches @ 50p), Swiss Chard (3 bunches @ 75p), Courgettes (2 @ 50p), Beetroot (2 bunches @ 75p), Apples (6 bags @ £1).
Harvest for tea room: 1 tray Onions, 1 Marrow.
Neil harvested for shop then picked Apples with Dave – 100kg Blenheim Orange picked from one tree! Will send to Pershore College for juicing. Val did various areas of weeding, sorted apples in fruit store etc. Diane cleared last of Courgette plants. Mary made a start on digging over the pig patch before rain got too heavy. Freda and Will cleared an area then planted a row of Brassicas, moved into glass house to weed Tomato bed and clear Basil. Weighed biggest pumpkin @ 15.9kg!

October 19th 2011, Wednesday Cold with sunny and showery spells; 11 eggs!
Staff: Deborah, Kate; *Volunteers:* Sylvia, Kathleen, Val, Marion, Rosemarie, John, Peter, Josh.
Peter removed turf and dug over soil to combine smaller Rhubarb bed with old Oriental Salad bed. Manured new bed. John cut a new corner bed in SE corner and started to dig it over – very hard ground. Sylvia and Josh removed old soil from Melon House bed and topped up with fresh loam. Marion planted out Thyme plants as edging to D1 and manured B3. Kathleen removed Crystal Lemon Cucumbers from cold frames and added loam to raise the soil level. Sowed 5 rows of winter lettuce. Sylvia sowed 4 rows of Rocket. Val collected Basil seed and potted on Pelargoniums to overwinter in cold frames. Sorted and sieved saved seeds.

October 19th 2012, Friday Dry and warm
Staff: Kate
Harvest for tea room: 1 tray Parsnips, 1 tray Lettuce, large bunch Chives.
Lifted last of Dahlias and put to dry in Vinery. Planted Crocosmia in Bothy Bed after digging out Artemisia and Symphitum. Continued weeding Pear borders, planting wallflowers and Scabious to fill the gaps. Also transplanted Penstemons.

October 2008

October 2009

October 2010

October 2011

October 2012

The Garden in Winter:
November, December and January

Now the garden really does begin to empty out, all apart from the hardiest winter vegetables that we can leave in the ground without fear of frost damage. We generally plant about a thousand leeks which keep the tea room in leek and potato soup from September through to the following March. They can stay in the ground as long as the infestation of leek moth is not too severe. Six hundred celeriac and a similar number of parsnips have to be lifted and stored in sand in the underground root store, in case the ground freezes over and we cannot dig them out. In the root store they sit happily in the cool and dark, awaiting the crackly radio request from the tea room for the next batch of soup. The lean-to glasshouses switch from summer crops to winter salads, providing a wide range of oriental mixed leaves throughout the coldest months. With no functioning boiler to heat the cast iron pipes that still run through all the glass houses we are reliant on the little bit of weak winter sun that gets reflected by the whitewashed back walls. The freestanding melon house does not have that advantage, so we have installed low voltage soil warming cables in the raised beds that keep it frost free during the winter months. Generally our diary entries get shorter and shorter as more time is spent indoors catching up on office work and drawing up plans for the following year.

If the weather is kind we can at least get on with preparing the ground for the year ahead. A frosty day might see us barrowing compost from the large bays behind the north wall, taking it to top dress the borders in the vegetable garden. A bonfire provides valuable wood ash to feed the apple trees and soft fruit, and the last of the fallen leaves are collected from around the park to add to our leaf mould cages. Valuable manure comes from neighbouring Home Farm, often in exchange for the service of mucking out their Victorian calf sheds which can only be done by hand. It is also the best time to dig over the ground, leaving the surface rough for the frost to break down. As Christmas approaches we collect greenery to create the wreaths and table arrangements for sale at Frost Fair. The log burner is a welcome addition to the Bothy which at this time of year doubles up as a potting shed, where Paperwhite Narcissi are put into terracotta pots ready to flower for Christmas.

In January much of our attention moves out into the orchard. On milder days we can continue the lengthy job of pruning the 160 trees that range in age from newly planted to almost a century old. For the first three winters we asked Seamus, the estate tree surgeon, to wield his chain saw. We then followed on with hand-held saws to thin congested branches. Now it is a question of keeping on top of the regrowth and trying to maintain a goblet shape. Our flock of rare breed chickens also enjoyed life in the orchard; that is until they became brave enough to raid the lunch boxes of unsuspecting picnickers. Banishing them to the woodland was a short-lived solution as the fox soon found them and began to pick them off in broad daylight. The depths of winter often finds Roger, our chief bean arch engineer, wielding loppers and mole grip to construct his latest edifice. These have improved year on year so that they are stronger and safer with elegant curved entrances that children love to run through at all times of year. The New Year is the best time to start forcing rhubarb under tall terracotta pots. These block out the light and absorb the warmth, encouraging the tender pink shoots so beloved of rhubarb connoisseurs.

November 4th	3 Savoys^{2} Lettuce^{1} 2 Red Cabbage^{6}		9
	– Russell 10 lb Potatoes^{5} 3 Savoys^{2} Lettuce^{1}		8
6	– Box of Flowers to Hon Miss Noel-Hill	1	
7	3 Brocoli^{3} Lettuce^{1} Celery^{2} 1/2 Cwt Potatoes$^{1/6}$ 1/4 Apples^{4}	2	4
	– Russell 10 lb Potatoes^{5} Lettuce^{1} Savoys^{2} 2 Celery^{2} 1/4 Apples^{3}	1	
11	10 lb Parsnips^{5} Lettuce^{1}		6
	– Russell 10 lb Potatoes^{5} Cabbage^{2} Lettuce^{1}		8
	a barrowfull of Carrots for the Horses	1	6
13	Box of Chrysanthemums & Violets to Hon Miss Noel Hill	1	
14	3 Brocoli^{3} 2 Savoys^{2} Lettuce^{1} 2 Celery^{2} 1/4 Apples^{2}		10
	Russell 10 lb Potatoes^{5} Savoys^{2} Lettuce^{1} Celery^{2} 1/4 Apples^{2}	1	
18	Cabbage^{2} Lettuce 1/2 Cwt Potatoes$^{1/6}$	1	9
	Russell 10 lb Potatoes^{5} Cabbage^{2} Red Cabbage^{2} Lettuce^{1}		10
20	Box of Chrysanthemums to Hon Miss Noel-Hill	1	
	Carried forward	14	10

November 19th 2008, Wednesday Sunny morning

Volunteers: John, Chris, Val and Derek.

Continued making path around Dahlia Border. Removed Alyssum, and dug out remaining sunflower stumps. Dug over plot 6.

November 19th 2009, Thursday

Volunteers: Derek, Ann, Sid, John, Phil.

Derek and Ann mulched Rhubarb bed. Phil and Derek edged Garlic bed. Dead-headed Polyanthus in Bothy Bed. Path weeding in Frame Yard. Sid painted wooden labels and brought in temporary boot scraper.

November 19th 2010, Friday Lovely sunny day; fog in the afternoon

Staff: Kate, Mary

Harvest for shop: 1 tray French Beans from Vinery.

Collected sample "Llanhydrock" vine eyes from blacksmith in Cound ready for wiring the walls – very convincing. Took to Walled Garden Meeting and got approval to go ahead with bulk order. New Espalier railings also approved of. Afternoon planting bulbs and perennials in new Espalier Border.

November 19th 2011, Saturday Dry and mild

Staff: DeborahVolunteers: Sheila, Helen, Peter, John, Paul

Harvest for shop: Brussels Sprouts (6 bags @ 75p), Mixed Salad Leaves 6 bags @ £1.50), Tomatoes (4 bags @ 75p), Swede (3 @ 75p, Leeks (6 @ £1), Sweet Peppers (2 bags @ 75p). 6 eggs.

Helen and Sheila harvested. Paul, Peter and John did a great job digging in the crimson clover in D2. Sheila planted 2 Rhubarb plants in Rhubarb bed and took remaining seed heads off the grazing rye, also cleaned out chickens. After lunch we all weeded the hoggin paths en masse.

November 19th 2012, Monday Dull weather and very quiet

Staff: Mary

Sorting and salad stuff. Sowed more lettuce in Tomato House. Brian came in to do bee feeding.

November 2008

November 2009

November 2011

November 2010

November 2012

1908	To Attingham Hall	£	s	d
November	Brought forward		14	10
21	3 Broccoli^{3} 3 Savoys^{2} Lettuce 2 Celery^{2} ½ Apples^{4}		1	
	Russell 10 lb Potatoes^{5} Savoys^{2} Lettuce Celery^{2} ½ Apples		1	
	White Chrysanthemums to Hon. A. Noel-Hill's Grape		1	
	3 Savoys^{2} Onions^{2}			4
	Russell 10 lb Potatoes^{5} Savoys^{2}			7
27	Box of Flowers to Hon. Miss Noel-Hill		1	
28	2 Broccoli^{2} Savoys^{2} Lettuce 2 Celery ½ Apples^{2}			9
	Russell 10 lb Potatoes^{5} Savoys^{2} Lettuce Celery^{2} ½ Apples		1	
		£ 1	1	6
December 2nd	Savoys^{2} Lettuce			3
	Russell 10 lb Potatoes^{5} Savoys^{2} Lettuce			8
4	Box of Flowers to Hon. Miss Noel-Hill		1	
5	4 lbs Apples Blenheim pippins			4
	Savoys^{2} 2 Broccoli^{4} 2 Celery^{2} Lettuce ½ Apples^{2}			9
	½ Cwt Potatoes		1	6
	Russell 10 lb Potatoes^{5} Savoys^{2} 2 Celery^{2} Lettuce ½ Apples		1	
9	Savoys^{2} Lettuce^{1}			3
	Russell 10 lb Potatoes^{5} Savoys^{2} Lettuce			8
11	Box of Flowers to Hon. Miss Noel-Hill		1	
12	3 Savoys^{2} 2 Broccoli^{2} Lettuce 2 Celery^{2} ½ Apples^{4}			11
	Russell 10 lb Potatoes^{5} Savoys^{2} Lettuce 2 Celery ½ Apples^{2}		1	
16	Savoys^{2} Lettuce ½ Cwt Potatoes 1/6		1	9
	Russell 10 lb Potatoes^{5} Savoys^{2} Lettuce			8
18	Box of Flowers to Hon. Miss Noel-Hill		1	
19	Savoys^{2} 2 Broccoli^{2} Lettuce 2 Celery^{2} ½ Apples^{4}			11
	Russell 10 lb Potatoes^{5} Savoys^{2} Lettuce 2 Celery^{2} ½ Apples		1	
23	Savoys^{2} Onions^{2} ½ Apples^{4} ½ B. Sprouts^{4}		1	
	Russell 10 lb Potatoes^{5} Onions^{2} ½ Apples^{2}			11
	Box of Flowers to Hon. Miss Noel-Hill		2	
26	2 Savoys^{2} 2 Broccoli^{3} Lettuce 2 Celery^{2} Apples^{2}			9
	Russell 10 lb Potatoes^{5} Savoys^{2} Lettuce Celery^{2} Apples^{2}		1	
	Carried forward	£ 1	—	4

December 19th 2008, Friday
Staff: Jenny
Harvest for shop: Brussels Sprouts, Leeks, Kale, Pumpkins, Parsley.
Took photos and video footage of garden.

December 19th 2009, Saturday Even colder overnight. Blue skies and sun
Staff: Kate; *Volunteers:* Sheila, Heather
Harvest for shop: Brussels Sprouts (9 stalks @ £1), Celeriac (5 @ £1)
Picked Sprouts by lopping stem and tidying. Digging Celeriac a hard job as ground very frozen. Sheila and Helen planted Anemones in Melon House bed, watered and mulched with Composted Green Waste. Sorted Gladioli bulbs and beans.

December 19th 2010, Sunday Very cold; 3" snow; very few visitors; 5 eggs!
Staff: Kate; *Volunteers:* Hedley.
Shovelled snow off paths. Sorted out Bothy for builders next week. Sorted out notice boards.

December 19th 2011, Monday Bleak wet day; 4 eggs
Staff: Mary, Deborah.
Harvest for shop: Brussels Sprouts (8 bags @ 75p), Eating Apples (3 bags @ £1), Cooking Apples (6 bags @ £1.50), Parsley (6 bags @ 75p), Seasonal stuffing herbs (6 bags @ £1), Florence Fennel (3 bags @ 75p), Sweet Peppers (8 bags @ £1), Chillies (4 bags @ £1.00, Butternut Squash (1 @ £2), Leeks (9 bunches @ 75p), Tomatoes (3 bags @ £1).
Took very last of the produce down to the shop. Planted out self seeded Claytonia. Sowed 3 rows lettuce in Vinery. Deborah fed fondant to the bees with Tony. Cyril and Graham continued excavating trench in orchard for electric cable. Caught 2 voles in the cold frames.

December 19th 2012, Wednesday Rain all day
Staff: Kate, Deborah, Mary, Jenny; *Volunteers:* Val, Jack
Harvest for tea room: 5kg Leeks.
Jenny dug leeks and found very bad infestation of Leek Moth (put waste on burning pile). Blue/Green Winter Hardy seem less susceptible. Val painted benches in the vinery. Jack finished making eeks for bee hives. Jenny started cutting down Delphiniums and Salvia patens in Pear Borders, then rained off. Meeting with Education team about next year's school visits. Prepared Bothy for filming tomorrow (John Cadwallader born in the Bothy in 1934). To Mytton and Mermaid for Christmas drinks!

December 2008

December 2009

December 2011

December 2010

December 2012

		£	s	d
1909	To Attingham Hall	£	s	d
January	Brought forward	2	4	3
	6 Apples^{2} 1lb Grapes$^{1/-}$ Filberts^{3}		1	5
12	2 Broccoli^{2} 2 Celery^{2} Mushrooms^{6}			10
	Parsley^{1} ½ Cwt Potatoes$^{1/6}$		1	7
13	¼ B. Sprouts^{2} 2 Broccoli^{2} 2 Celery^{2} Lettuce^{1}			7
	Endive^{1} Mustard & Cress^{1} Parsley^{1} Mushrooms^{4}			7
	6 Apples^{2} 1¼lb Grapes$^{1/3}$ Flowers 2/-		3	5
	– Russell 10lb Potatoes^{5} Greens^{3}			8
14	¼ B. Sprouts^{2} 2 Broccoli^{2} Celery^{2} Lettuce^{1}			7
	Mustard & Cress^{1} Parsley^{1} Rhubarb^{3} 6 Apples^{2} lb Grapes$^{1/-}$		1	7
15	½ Mushrooms^{4} 2 Celery^{2} 1¼lb Grapes$^{1/3}$		1	9
16	½ B. Sprouts^{4} 5 Broccoli^{5} 4 Celery^{4} Herbs^{3}		1	4
	1 Dz Lettuce^{4} Endive^{4} Mustard & Cress^{1}			9
	½ Cwt Potatoes$^{1/6}$ lb Mushrooms^{8} Seakale^{4}		2	6
	Rhubarb^{4} 1 Peck Apples^{8} 12 Apples^{6} 1lb Grapes$^{1/-}$		2	6
	– Russell 10lb Potatoes^{5} Kale^{3} Celery^{2} ¼ Apples^{2}		1	
18	2 Broccoli^{2} Mushrooms^{6} 2 Celery^{2} Cucumber^{4}		1	2
	Mustard & Cress^{1} Parsley^{1} 1 Dz Beetroots^{8}			10
	6 Apples^{2} 1½ lb Grapes$^{1/6}$		1	8
19	2 Broccoli^{2} ¼ B. Sprouts^{2} 2 Celery^{2} Lettuce			7
	Endive^{1} Mustard & Cress^{1} Parsley^{1} ½ Cwt Potatoes$^{1/6}$		1	9
	lb Mushrooms^{8} 6 Apples^{2} 1lb Grapes$^{1/-}$		1	10
20	Mushrooms^{6} Celery^{2} Parsley^{1}			9
	– Russell 10lb Potatoes^{5} Savoy^{3}			8
21	2 Broccoli^{2} Celery^{2} 12 Parsnips^{5} Mushrooms^{6}		1	3
	Mustard & Cress^{1} Rhubarb^{4} 6 Apples^{2} 1¼lb Grapes$^{1/3}$		1	10
22	Mushrooms^{6} 12 Apples^{3} 2lb Grapes$^{2/-}$		2	9
23	2 Broccoli^{2} Celery^{2} ½ Apples^{4}			8
	– Russell 10lb Potatoes^{5} Celery^{2} 2 Kale^{4} ¼ Apples^{2}		1	1
27	Greens^{3} ½ Cwt Potatoes$^{1/6}$		1	9
	– Russell 10lb Potatoes^{5} Greens^{3}			8
29	box of Flowers to Hon Miss Noel-Hill		2	
	Carried forward	£ 4	6	7

January 20th 2009, Tuesday Beautiful sunny day, clouding over in afternoon

Staff: Jenny; *Volunteers:* David, Alan, Neil, Denise, Mary, Sue, Steve, Pam, Kath

Very productive day. Shifted turf along path back to make all wall beds the same. Lifted turf on remaining patches around wall. Dug over most of plot 4. Also fed deer in the afternoon as Colin on a course.

January 19th 2010, Tuesday Overcast but not too cold

Staff: Kate; *Volunteers:* Neil, Denise

Harvest for tea room: 15kg Leeks .

Orchard pruning: Seamus back with chainsaw and chipper. Did three more big trees: Bramley, Lord Lambourn and Newton Wonder. Logged and chipped all the waste. Dumped half inside the Walled Garden and half outside for path making. Denise cleared celery and lettuces from ornamental bed, also Endives (Cornet de Bordeaux completely frosted). Neil had a big bonfire and dug 45 leeks for tea room.

January 19th 2011, Wednesday Heavy frost then fog

Staff: Kate, Katherine; *Volunteers:* Roger, Ray, Ann, Ivor

Snowdrops out in the woodland! Pruning in orchard with Seamus. Started on next third: Laxton Superb, Shropshire Pippin, Mere de Menage, Annie Elizabeth, James Grieve, Ashmead's Kernal, Cox's Orange Pippin, Rival, Lord Derby. Also contractors in collecting leaves from the park and dumping in cages in orchard. Val sowed 120 jiffy pots of Super Aquadulce Broad Beans, put on heated beds in glasshouse. This should do 2 double rows across the Legume bed.

January 19th 2012 Thursday Showery but sunny in afternoon; getting colder

Staff: Kate, Gaye; *Volunteers:* Chris, Tony, Wendy, Belinda, Ray, Ivor, Derek, Simon, Roger, Felicity

Tony pressure sprayed inside of Melon house prior to repainting with lime wash. Chris layed last soil warming cable and covered lightly with loam. Wendy and Felicity weeded garlic and onions. Belinda sowed winter lettuce in Pinery and transplanted seedlings. Chaps finished digging new edge bed and laying turf on new path through nut walk. Chris painted more labels and mulched New Bothy Bed with leaf mould. Gaye and Kate orchard pruning. Cut Chrysanthemums from greenhouse to decorate Bothy.

January 19th 2013 Snow settled; cold grey day

Staff: Mary

The snow made it impossible to do any gardening today. So it was decided that better use of my time could be made with continuing with a painting project for the Walled Garden.

January 2009

January 2010

January 2011

January 2012

January 2013

The Garden in Spring: *February, March, April*

The first flowers to emerge in the parkland are the snowdrops, swathes of scented double white blooms that usually appear around Valentine's Day. For the last three years we have lit the Mile Walk with hundreds of lanterns, leading the way to the floodlit snow drops and the Bothy which becomes a cosy venue for mulled wine and apple juice. Iris reticulata also brave the wintry weather shining like jewels in the frame ground pots and flower beds. Spring starts early for us in the Walled Garden, at least when it comes to sowing seeds in the glasshouse. We tend to begin in the melon house as that is where we have our heated propagating mats which get the young seedlings off to a very speedy start. Cucumbers can germinate in less than 48 hours, as can melons and tomatoes, then setting the pace for pricking out, potting on and a constant search for more space. A cosy warm glasshouse full of tasty seeds is also an attractive spot for unwelcome visitors such as mice and voles. Barricades of glass, wire and plastic help keep them out of the seed trays, whilst Mary's skills in rodent control have kept numbers down over the last couple of years. Outside it is still far too cold to consider sowing much apart from parsnips, so we concentrate on soil preparation and getting the paths edged, weeded and looking at their best. Out in the nut walk we have been coppicing the hazel, cutting it right down to ground level to ensure the regrowth is straight and tall for more bean poles. The shorter twiggy growth we use for pea sticks, hanging the bundles along the walls until they are needed.

By March, the broad beans (sown in recycled paper pots to avoid the depredations of the pheasants) have been hardened off and are ready to be planted out into the open ground. This follows an anxious time of gradually acclimatising them to outdoor conditions: beginning by pushing them out into the fresh air like so many babies in prams, bringing them in at the hint of a chill wind. As they grow on they are sent out to play, even if the weather is brisk, ending up even risking a sleepover outside before being eased out of the glasshouse nest into the chilly legume bed with only a fleecy comfort blanket if the weather turns frosty. Potatoes, on the other hand, sit snugly in their egg box cradles on the Bothy windowsills. There they wait to chit in the sunlight, growing sturdy shoots to get them off to a flying start when we finally plant them at the end of the month. The fan trained fruit on the South wall begins to flower and we hope that late frosts don't damage the blossom. Georgian gardeners had the luxury of firing up the heated walls if frost threatened, but we can only keep our fingers crossed.

In April the apple trees in the orchard start to blossom, tempting the bees to emerge from their hibernation to pollinate the fruit. We also emerge from the glass houses and switch from indoor sowing to using the outdoor seed bed in the Frame Ground. Here the lettuce, leeks and cabbages are sown in relative comfort, sheltered from the chilly winds of the main garden and protected from the birds by means of bent wire cages. Now is the really lean time of year when it comes to harvesting: the "Hungry Gap" of old gardening books. The last of the parsnips and carrots have been taken out of the root store, only the hardiest of greens have pulled through in the garden. Kale, chard and purple sprouting broccoli make a tasty addition to a meal while the first radishes and spring onions are ready in the cold frames. The flower borders are much more productive, with all the spring bulbs diverting attention from the acres of bare earth. Daffodils, early tulips and hyacinths glow with colour while the fresh young foliage of herbaceous perennials makes a wonderful foil to the gaudy display.

PARSNIP Tender and True
Peach

		£	s	d
1909	To Attingham Hall	£	s	d
January	Brought forward	4	6	7
30	4 Broccoli[4] 2 Celery[2] Onions[2] ½ apples[4]		1	
	2o Russell 10lb Potatoes[5] Scotch Kale[4] Celery[2] ¼ apples[2]		1	1
	£	4	8	8
February 3rd	Savoys[2] Carrots & Parsnips[4]			6
	To Russell 10lb Potatoes[5] Savoys[2]			7
5	Box of Flowers to Hon Miss Noel-Hill		1	6
6	4 Broccoli[6] 2 Celery[2] ½ apples[4]		1	
	- Russell 10lb Potatoes[5] Scotch Kale[4] 2 Celery[2] ¼ Apples[2]		1	1
10	6 Scotch Kale[4] ½ Cwt Potatoes[1/6]		1	10
	- Russell 10lb Potatoes[5] Greens[2]			7
12	- Box of Flowers to Hon Miss Noel-Hill		1	6
13	4 Broccoli[6] 2 Celery[2] Rhubarb[3] ½ apples[2]		1	1
	- Russell 10lb Potatoes[5] Scotch Kale[4] 2 Celery[2] ¼ apples[2]		1	1
17	1 Dz Parsnips[4]			4
	- Russell 10lb Potatoes[5] 1 Dz Parsnips[4]			9
19	Box of Flowers to Hon Miss Noel-Hill		1	6
20	6 Scotch Kale[4] 2 Celery[2] ½ apples[4]			10
	- Russell 10lb Potatoes[5] Scotch Kale[4] 2 Celery[2] ¼ apples[2]		1	1
24	6 Scotch Kale[4] Peck Potatoes[6]			10
	- Russell 10lb Potatoes[5] 6 Scotch Kale[4]			9
26	Box of Flowers to Hon Miss Noel-Hill		1	6
27	6 Scotch Kale[4] 2 Celery[2] ½ Cwt Potatoes[1/6] ½ apples[4]		2	4
	- Russell 10lb Potatoes[5] 6 Scotch Kale[4] 2 Celery[2] ¼ apples[2]		1	1
	£	1	1	9
March 3rd	1 Dz Parsnips[4] Onions[2]			6
	- Russell 10lb Potatoes[5] Parsnips[4] Onions[2]			11
5	Box of Flowers to Hon Miss Noel-Hill		1	6
6	Scotch Kale[4] Celery[2] ½ apples[4]			10
	- Russell 10lb Potatoes[5] Scotch Kale[4] Celery[2] ¼ apples[2]		1	1
10	1 Dz Parsnips[4] 1 Dz Beetroot[6]			10
	- Russell 10lb Potatoes[5] Parsnips[4]			9
	Carried forward		6	5

February 19th 2009, Thursday Overcast mild day

No *Staff*: (Jenny's last day on 13th February. Kate to start on 16th March).
Continued digging over patch 5. Swept Bothy.

February 19th 2010, Friday

Staff: Kate
Sowed more salads in glass house. Pricked out Nicotiana.

February 19th 2011, Saturday Dull and cloudy but lots of visitors.

Staff: Kate; *Volunteers*: Sheila, Paul, Fiona
Harvest for shop: Jerusalem artichokes (4 bags @ £1) Snowdrops (10 pots @ £4), Iris "Harmony" (5 pots @ £4), Narcissi "Tête à Tête" (9 pots @ £4).
Harvest for tearoom: 1 tray mixed salad.
Sheila picked salad and dug artichokes. Fiona painted blackboards then moved leaves from heap into new cage. Paul put cages over broad beans (against pheasants) and pea sticks over Feltham First peas which are now showing. I did another snowdrop walk. Then put seed potatoes into egg trays to chit on attic window sills in Bothy.

February 19th 2012, Sunday Dry. Snowfall over night. Snow drops at their peak in the park. Lots of visitors

Staff: Deborah; *Volunteers*: Hedley, Gaynor, Irene.
Gaynor and Irene potted up bare rooted herbaceous plants in the Bothy. Lots of visitors coming in to chat. Hedley lit the fire, watered the glasshouses, continued low hazel fencing, cleaned out the chickens. Deborah started training new cherry trees.

February 19th 2013, Tuesday Lovely sunny day, heaving with visitors

Staff: Kate, Mary, Jenny; *Volunteers*: Sally, Helen, Ann, Denise, Diane, Zac, Val.
Took 70 pots of snowdrops to the shop: selling fast. Trusty Tuesday event: children potting up daffodils. Sold out by 2pm having potted 90 @ £4 each.
Everyone weeded around circular flower beds, all four now planted up, looking very smart. Zac sawed up logs for Bothy log burner then helped Val weed behind sweet pea fence. Mary pricked out chilli plants. Kate cut back pear borders and hoed D2

February 2009

February 2011

February 2010

February 2012

February 2013

14

1909	To Attingham H	£	s	d
March	Brought forward		6	5
12	Box of Flowers to Hon. Miss Noel-Hill		1	6
13	Scotch Kale^{4} 2 Celery^{2} ½ Cwt Potatoes$^{1/6}$ Apples^{4}		2	4
	– Russell 10 lb Potatoes^{5} Scotch Kale^{4} Celery^{2} Apples^{2}		1	1
17	Carrots and Parsnips^{4}			4
	– Russell 10 lb Potatoes^{5} Parsnips^{4}			9
19	Box of Flowers to Hon. Miss Noel-Hill		1	6
20	Scotch Kale^{4} Celery^{2} ½ Apples^{4}			10
	– Russell 10 lb Potatoes^{5} Scotch Kale^{4} Celery^{2} ¼ Apples^{2}		1	1
24	Greens^{2} – Russell 10 lb Potatoes^{5} Greens^{2}			9
26	Box of Flowers to Hon. Miss Noel-Hill		1	6
27	½ B. Sprouts^{4} ½ Cwt Potatoes$^{1/6}$ Celery^{2} ½ Apples^{4}		2	4
	– Russell 10 lb Potatoes^{4} Scotch Kale^{4} Celery^{2} ¼ Apples^{2}		1	
31	Kale^{3} – Russell 10 lb Potatoes^{4} Kale^{3}			10
		£ 1	2	3

March 19th 2009, Thursday Very foggy to start but warm and sunny by midday

Staff: Kate (day 4, having started on March 16th); *Volunteers:* John, Sid
Harvest for shop: Purple Sprouting Broccoli (12 bunches @ 50p), Curly Kale (6 bunches @ 50p), Lettuce (4 @ 75p).
Harvest for tearoom: Chives and Parsley (for cheese scones).
John put up another bean pole structure on Plot 5 using hazel coppiced from nut walk. Sid finished digging garlic patch. Kate planted four more double rows of Garlic "Casablanca", almost all in now. Also had tour of whole Estate with Ron and fed deer in Deer Park.

March 18th 2010, Thursday

Staff: Kate; *Volunteers:* Roger, Mary, Jason, Phil, John, Ray
Interviewing again for new Seasonal gardeners, but lots done by volunteers. Mary picked salads and took down to tea room. Roger and Jason did more manure clearing from calf sheds at Home Farm (dumped by tractor just inside walled garden to mulch wall borders. Phil, John and Ray weeded surface of dug beds. Roger and Jason then made two sweet pea wigwams in Frame Yard at end of Ben's allotment.

March 19th 2011, Saturday Frosty start but beautiful day. Many visitors as free admission weekend!

Staff: Mary; *Volunteers:* Sheila, Heather and Paul
Harvest for shop: Mixed salad leaves (12 bags @ 75p), Jerusalem Artichokes (3 bags @ 75p)
Sheila and Heather transplanted pea plants from Tomato House to ornamental arch and then barricaded them in with pea sticks. Likewise for the existing "Kelvedon Wonder" peas in B1, re-sowed in gaps created by bird foraging. Paul did a big chunk of refining bed in B4 with rake. Mary made a start on sowing oriental salads in bed along North facing wall.

March 19th 2012, Monday Cold night, sunny most of the day

Staff: Kate, Mary, Deborah
A day of catching up and meetings. Deborah did some bee keeping work, Mary worked on Cabinet of Curiosities in Bothy. Kate watered greenhouses, sorted out hoses and sowed more annual flowers and herbs in Melon House bed.

March 19th 2013, Tuesday Dull and cold in the morning, sunny afternoon

Staff: Kate, Jenny, Laura; *Volunteers:* Neil, Denise, Helen, Sally, Ann, Val, Hannah, James.
Neil tidied manure spilling out of compost heap after four trailer loads delivered from Home Farm. Two bays now full, but more still to be mucked out of calf shed. Neil, Jenny, Laura and Hannah got the first shift. Kate, Ann, Sally and James did the second. Extremely smelly and heavy job. Chocolate cake for Hannah's 18th birthday. Removed ash from bonfire to top dress around orchard trees. Jenny then coaxed it back into life and burned last of hazel brash and weed pile. Laura pricked out Campanula seedlings that she had sown last month as well as sowed more parsnips with Hannah. Denise and Val weeded around base of apple trees, then more edging. Kate potted up Dahlias that had been over-wintered in the attic.

March 2009

March 2010

March 2012

March 2011

March 2013

		s	d
April 2nd	Box of Flowers to Hon Miss Noel-Hill	1	6
3	½ B. Sprouts 4 2 Celery 2 ½ apples 4		10
	– Russell 10 lb Potatoes 4 Celery 2 Kale 3 ¼ apples		11
7	Carrots 3 Parsnips 3 onions 2		8
	– Russell 10 lb Potatoes 4 Parsnips 3 onions 2		9
8	Box of Flowers to Hon Miss Noel-Hill	1	
10	B. S. Tops 4 ½ Cwt Potatoes 1/6 Rhubarb 3 ¼ apples 2	2	3
	– Russell 10 lb Potatoes 4 B.S. Tops 3 Rhubarb 3 ¼ apples 2	1	
14	Scotch Kale 4		4
	– Russell 10 lb Potatoes 4 Scotch Kale 4		8
16	Box of Flowers to Hon Miss Noel-Hill	2	
	Greens 3 Lettuce 2 Rhubarb 3		8
	– Russell 10 lb Potatoes 4 Greens 3 Lettuce Rhubarb 3		11
21	Scotch Kale 3 Lettuce		4
	– Russell 10 lb Potatoes 4 Scotch Kale 3 Lettuce		8
23	Box of Flowers to Hon Miss Noel Hill	1	6
24	Scotch Kale 4 Lettuce 2 ½ Cwt Potatoes 1/6 Rhubarb 3 apples 2	2	5
	Carried forward	18	5

April 18th 2009, Saturday Cool and dry

Staff: Kate; *Volunteers:* Helen and Jay

Harvest for shop: Chard (12 bunches @ 50p), Spring Onion (6 bunches @ 50p), Rhubarb (3 bunches @ 75p). Began digging up yellow chard as beginning to bolt, put on compost heap. Started laying cardboard on plot 4 (from Shropshire Star presses via John) and spreading with compost mulch to try to smother bindweed.

April 19th 2010, Monday Overcast, some sun in the afternoon

Staff: Kate, Deborah; *Volunteers:* Elfriede

Harvest for shop: Radish (11 bunches @ 50p), Lettuce (6 @ 50p), Forced Rhubarb (4 @ £1), Tulip "Purissima", "Negrita" and "Zurel" (3 bunches @ £2), Narcissi "Poeticus" and "Cheerfulness" (3 bunches @ £2).

Harvest for tea room: 1 tray Radish, Rocket and Mixed Salad.

Elfriede picked flowers for vases and for shop, also did lots of watering. Deborah ordered blackboards for garden and trolleys for produce sales in the shop. I planted Delphiniums and Sweet peas in New Bothy bed. Sprayed seedlings in seed bed and Melon House with seaweed concentrate.

Interviewed Katherine for Women Returners to Amenity Gardening Scheme apprenticeship – another member of staff!

April 19th 2011, Tuesday Perfect sunny day: teeming with visitors

Staff: Mary, Deborah; *Volunteers:* Anne, Amanda, Alex, Diane, Denise, Val, Neil, Linda, Jackie.

Harvest for tea room: 1 tray Lettuce, Sage and Chives.

Neil dug over outside South wall under Peach trees. Amanda, Alex, Deborah and Linda dug over most of C3. Anne earthed up many rows of potatoes. Linda weeded. Alex sowed more parsley along edge of ornamental bed. Denise and Val thoroughly weeded legumes in B4. Jackie weeded new flower border along main path, as well as Bothy Bed. Children came up to plant potatoes for Trusty Tuesday event. About 40 potatoes planted and many pots of peas sown for the children to take away.

Tulips stunning throughout the garden – much admired by visitors.

April 19th 2012, Thursday Heavy showers then sun; cold enough to light log burner in the Bothy

Staff: Kate, Mary, Gaye; *Volunteers:* Wendy, Tony, Chris, Ray, John, Felicity, Simon.

Ray and Simon planted last of potatoes on the "Dark Side" (an experiment to see how they might grow in shade of North Wall). John put new electric fence up for pigs (arrived on April 2nd and already ploughed up a quarter of their area!) and mowed the paths in the new quarter. Felicity weeded frame yard edges. Chris pricked out lobelia into modules also sowed courgettes. Ray finished planting out "Greenshaft" peas in B3. Wendy planted out Calabrese in C1. Felicity and Gaye cleared tulips out of raised beds and planted ranunculus (White, "Picotee Pink", "Pauline's Purple"). Felicity planted Gladioli bulbs in cutting bed.

April 19th 2013, Friday Lovely calm sunny day

Staff: Kate, Belinda

4.8kg forced rhubarb picked for tearoom, also salads from glasshouse. Belinda sowed 11 varieties of lettuce in the new seed bed then planted two rows of lettuce in A3. I planted 30 tomatoes in ring culture pots in the Vinery, using a mixture of compost, mole hill soil and Composted Green Waste. Watered all the glasshouses then planted another row of Anya potatoes in A3. Cleared bolted rocket and mustard greens from Tomato House and fed to pigs - not that impressed! They are beginning to dig and getting a lot more vocal. Suddenly noticed the lids of the forcers were being pushed off and found wonderful tender pink stems ready to pick. Has spring finally begun?

April 2009

April 2011

April 2010

April 2012

April 2013

Postscript and Acknowledgements

The gardener's log has now come full circle, the end of five years of experiment and adventure. We have learnt from our mistakes, and although the whole garden is not finished (which garden ever is?) we now have a template to follow which seems to work for us. We made the decision right at the outset that this was to be an evolution rather than a revolution, bringing visitors along with the process of transforming a garden rather than beavering away behind closed doors and then revealing the finished article. A six year rotation forces us to plan well ahead, and with one quarter left to cultivate we feel we are very nearly there. If we keep our nerve and don't overstretch ourselves I predict we will be putting the pigs into the final quarter in time to celebrate our next birthday. Hopefully we will soon have a garden of which even Mr Atkinson would have been proud.

Acknowledgements
Many people have helped in the production of this booklet, just as with the restoration of the garden, and sadly there is not the space to thank them all. However, special mention must be made of Mary Rickards, whose exquisite illustrations bring all the text to life, of Deborah Simmonds who took many of the photographs herself, and of the staff, volunteers and friends who have proffered the remaining pictures. My special thanks go to Bob, Mark, Sarah and Ben who have supported the restoration from the word go, as well as all the volunteers who have made the whole enterprise possible and so enjoyable. Finally I must thank my family, all of whom have volunteered in the garden at various points, not from any particular horticultural interest, but in order to see me from time to time!

Kate Nicoll

Aerial shot 2013 (photography by www.skylens.co.uk)